Topics in British Politics

The Politics of Northern Ireland

Raymond Mullan

LONGMAN GROUP LIMITED
Longman House
Burnt Mill, Harlow, Essex

First published 1986
ISBN 0 582 34316 X

Set in 11/12 pt. Garamond (Stempel), Linotron 202

Produced by Longman Group (F.E. Limited)
Printed in Hong Kong

To Geraldine

Acknowledgements
We are grateful to the following for permission to reproduce photographs: Belfast News Letter, page 29; Belfast Telegraph, pages 2, 5, 25, 30 (photo: Charles Cockcroft), 35, 37 (photo: Roy Smyth); Camera Press, page 7 (photo: S. Szebelledy); The Guardian, page 42 (photo: Denis Thorpe); Irish News, pages 32 (photo: Gerry Casey), 45 (photo: Brendan Murphy); Northern Ireland Office, page 22; Pacemaker Press International, pages 11, 16, 17, 18, 21, 23, 36, 38, 40, 43, 46, 48; Popperfoto, page 8; Press Association, page 57; Rex Features Ltd, page 51; Topham, page 56; Sporting Pictures (UK) Ltd, page 6.

Contents

Abbreviations

BBC	British Broadcasting Corporation
CND	Campaign for Nuclear Disarmament
DUP	Democratic Unionist Party
INLA	Irish National Liberation Army
IRA	Irish Republican Army
ITV	Independent Television
NATO	North Atlantic Treaty Organisation
NICRA	Northern Ireland Civil Rights Association
NORAID	Northern Aid
OUP	Official Unionist Party
RUC	Royal Ulster Constabulary
SDP	Social Democratic Party (in Britain)
SDLP	Social Democratic and Labour Party (in Northern Ireland)
UDA	Ulster Defence Association
UDR	Ulster Defence Regiment
UFF	Ulster Freedom Fighters
UVF	Ulster Volunteer Force

1   The roots of conflict

The problem of violent community conflict in Northern Ireland has been a continuous element in British and Irish politics since the outbreak of the present troubles in 1969. The problem has lasted so long, not only because it is so complicated, but also because its roots go back for centuries.

The Ulster Plantation

A good starting point when examining the problem is the British colonisation, or plantation, of Ulster in the seventeenth century. English governments had been trying to conquer Ireland for centuries with only limited success. But in 1603 a major uprising, led by the Ulster Gaelic chieftain, Hugh O'Neill, was finally defeated by English troops. This gave King James I of England an opportunity to secure this most rebellious part of Ireland for the British Crown by placing large numbers of loyal English and Scottish settlers on the lands of the defeated Ulstermen.

The native Irish, who had been evicted from their lands, resented the new settlers, and in a number of rebellions attempted to drive them out. Ultimately they failed and at the Battle of the Boyne (1690) the last great Gaelic Irish rebellion was decisively crushed by the armies of William of Orange – King William III. The Battle of the Boyne thus confirmed the permanence of the Ulster Plantation.

Most of the new settlers were lowland Scots who, unlike most English settlers in Ireland, already had a strong historic association with Ulster which was separated from Scotland by only 32 kilometres of sea at the closest point. The new settlers therefore felt at home in Ulster and were determined to stay.

In time the hostility between the native Irish and the planters might have disappeared as intermarriage and social interaction took place. A major obstacle to this, however, was the Protestant religion of the new settlers which set them apart from the Catholicism of the native Irish. In particular, the Presbyterianism of the lowland Scots made them regard the Roman Catholic Church with loathing and contempt. And so two quite distinct and mutually hostile communities became established in Ulster.

The people of Northern Ireland have long historical memories. The Protestant victory of King William of Orange in 1690 is celebrated every twelfth of July.

Partition

The scale of the Ulster Plantation and the religion of the new settlers helped to give Ulster an identity quite distinct from the rest of Ireland. It was substantially Protestant and English-speaking and it developed a more prosperous pattern of agriculture. More importantly, in the nineteenth century, north-east Ulster was the only part of Ireland to become industrialised with the development of shipbuilding and linen manufacture. Belfast was transformed from a small town into a major industrial city which looked to Liverpool and London rather than to Dublin for its prosperity.

Towards the end of the nineteenth century a nationalist campaign backed by the majority of Irish voters began to persuade the British Liberal Government to grant Ireland a limited form of independence, called *Home Rule*. The reaction of Ulster Protestants was to form the Ulster Unionist Council which later became the Ulster Unionist Party. Its object was to oppose Home Rule and to maintain the union of Ireland with Britain.

Ulster Unionists opposed Home Rule partly because, unlike the rest of Ireland, Ulster's prosperity was closely linked with access to the markets of the British Empire. This could be threatened by an independent Ireland. Also, Protestants did not welcome the thought of being a minority in what they believed would be a state dominated by the Roman Catholic Church. The unionist fears for their religious and civil liberties were expressed in the cry 'Home Rule is Rome Rule!'.

While Irish nationalist opinion was becoming impatient for self-government, by 1913 Ulster Unionists were preparing to resist Home Rule by force if necessary. Civil war between North and South was only avoided by the outbreak of the First World War in 1914 and by the eventual partition of Ireland in 1920.

The Government of Ireland Act (1920) gave Home Rule to Ireland, but to satisfy the objections of the Ulster Unionists six of the nine Ulster counties were to have their own separate parliament and government in Belfast. Though intended to pave the way for an eventual united Ireland under Home Rule, the provisions of the 1920 Act were reluctantly accepted by the Ulster Unionists only as a means of saving themselves from Dublin rule. Thus was the state of Northern Ireland born.

Two communities

The boundaries of Northern Ireland were drawn in such a way that the Protestants and unionists would be in a majority and thus feel secure. It was to be their state. But the new state also included a large minority of Catholics who were mostly nationalists and had opposed partition. In other words the new Northern Ireland state contained not one community but two.

Northern Ireland Protestants regard themselves as British and are proud of it. The British Royal Family and the Union Jack are powerful symbols of that identity, much as they are in Britain. But whereas in Britain such symbols are sources of unity, in Northern

Ulster in 1914. This division of Ulster into areas of unionist and nationalist support corresponded to the main concentrations of Protestant and Catholic settlement. The pattern remains largely unchanged.

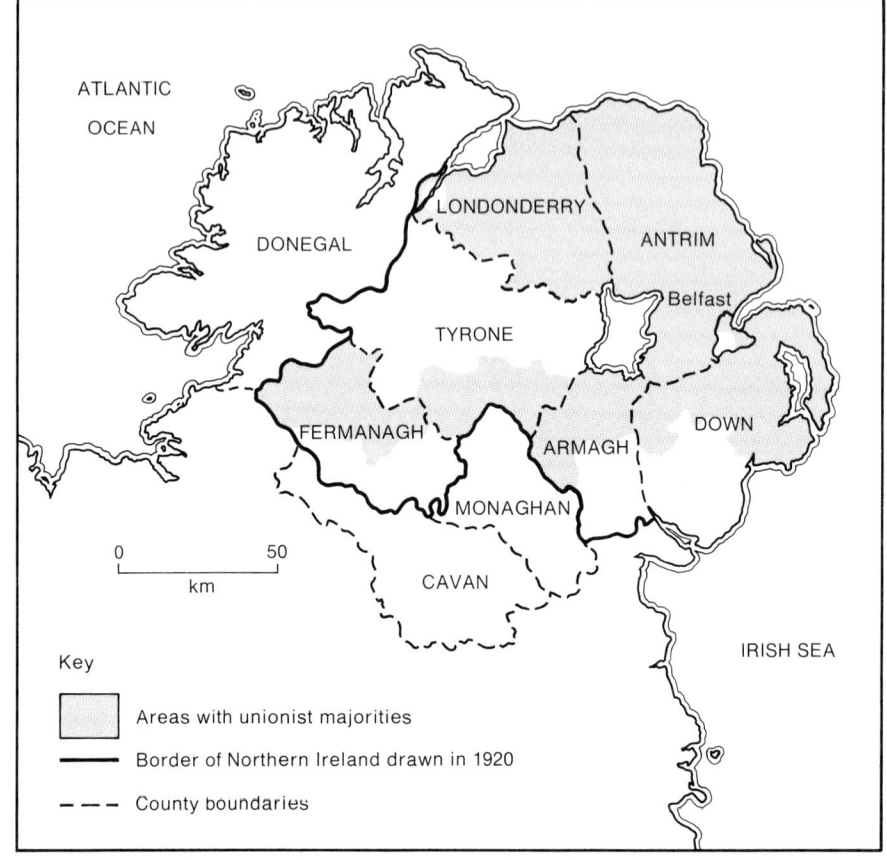

ATLANTIC OCEAN

DONEGAL

LONDONDERRY

ANTRIM

Belfast

TYRONE

FERMANAGH

ARMAGH

DOWN

MONAGHAN

CAVAN

IRISH SEA

0   50
km

Key

Areas with unionist majorities

Border of Northern Ireland drawn in 1920

County boundaries

Ireland they are symbols of division, of belonging to a 'Loyalist' or unionist community. This is best demonstrated on 12 July when Protestants wearing 'English' bowler hats and carrying British Union Jacks parade to celebrate the Protestant victory of William of Orange in 1690.

Northern Ireland Catholics, on the other hand, regard themselves as Irish and have no emotional attachment to the union with Britain. Like the people of the Irish Republic they usually refer to Northern Ireland as 'the North' or 'the Six Counties' to emphasise that their country is 'Ireland'. They never refer to it as Ulster, for that is the name of the historic province, three of whose counties are not included in Northern Ireland.

Community divisions in Northern Ireland, however, are not confined to political loyalties. Though a good deal of social contact does take place between Protestants and Catholics most people in Northern Ireland live in areas that are predominantly Protestant or predominantly Catholic. Most of Counties Antrim and Down are overwhelmingly Protestant, while West Belfast, the city of

Protestants and Catholics unite to welcome Barry McGuigan back to Belfast after he had won the World Featherweight Boxing Championship.

Londonderry (called 'Derry' by most Catholics) and the border areas are overwhelmingly Catholic. In these areas there would be little contact between Protestants and Catholics, thus increasing the sense of two separate communities.

Another feature of the social division is the fact that Protestants and Catholics go to different schools. Most of the Protestants actually go to state schools many of which fly the Union Jack. Catholics prefer to attend schools built and managed by the Catholic Church.

The main difference between Catholic and state schools is that in the former religion plays a much more important role in the life of the school, particularly at the primary level. Catholic Church teaching is not only taught in religion classes; all teachers, most of whom are Catholic, are expected to promote Catholic moral values at all times. In the state schools religion is less prominent although there is Bible instruction.

There are other differences between the schools and these reflect the wider cultural differences between the two communities. State schools, for example, make little attempt to foster an interest in Gaelic sports, Irish language or Irish history before the Plantation. Instead they promote 'British' culture, including games like cricket. Generally

Hurling is a traditional Irish sport, but it is played in Northern Ireland only in the Catholic community. Unionists regard it as foreign to their British culture.

speaking, Catholic schools make a much greater effort to give expression to Catholics' sense of 'Irishness'.

It is debatable whether separate schooling reinforces the social divisions or simply reflects them. In any case it is a fact of life in Northern Ireland and is the most visible symbol of the existence of two separate communities.

Topics for discussion

1 What do Ulster Protestants celebrate on 12 July?
2 Find out about the religious beliefs of Roman Catholics and Protestants. How do they differ from each other?
3 Why were Ulster Unionists opposed to Irish Home Rule?
4 Why do you think that the whole of Ulster was not included in the new Northern Ireland in 1920?
5 Do you think that partition was a good solution to the Ulster problem? What would you have done if you were the British prime minister at the time? What problems does partition create?
6 Do you think that religiously integrated (or mixed) schools would work in Northern Ireland? Give reasons.

2 Government

All communities are faced with problems, like security or welfare, which require actions or decisions to be taken on behalf of the community as a whole. This may involve matters like deciding how to deal with anti-social behaviour or drawing up plans for the provision of medical care. Such actions and decisions form the basis of the work of government.

The difficulty with government in Northern Ireland is that there are two communities. Between 1921 and 1972 the Government of Northern Ireland was controlled by the Unionist Party elected by the majority Protestant community. Since the views of the Catholic minority were not represented in government, and Catholic loyalty to the new state was also suspect, government became the rule by the one community over the other.

Majority Rule: Stormont 1921–68

The Government of Ireland Act of 1920 established a government and parliament in Northern Ireland to deal with purely local matters. The British Government kept responsibility for defence, foreign relations, trade and the regulation of the economy. But in most other matters, including law and order, the new Northern Ireland Government, located at Stormont Castle on the outskirts of Belfast, was left to develop its own laws and policies with little interference from London.

The path to Stormont, symbol of Protestant power. It was from here that unionists governed Northern Ireland for fifty-one years.

Eamon De Valera (1882–1975) was the leader of the Southern Government during the Irish War of Independence (1919–22). He spent most of the war in the USA raising money for the IRA. He refused to accept the 1921 Treaty which ended the war and led to the present partition of Ireland. With the Fianna Fail Party which he founded he was committed to the creation of a completely independent Irish Republic which would include the whole of Ireland. In 1937, when he was Prime Minister of the Southern Irish Free State, he renamed it 'Eire', or Ireland, making clear the South's claim over Northern Ireland. He was regarded with the deepest hostility by Northern unionists.

The new state was immediately attacked by the Irish Republican Army (IRA), which opposed partition, and Dublin governments, particularly under Eamon De Valera, did not conceal their desire to remove the border and end the North's union with Britain. Moreover, within Northern Ireland there existed a substantial Catholic minority which shared these nationalist aspirations and could not be relied upon to be loyal to the unionist state.

In these circumstances the policies of the unionist governments of Northern Ireland were dominated by attempts to maintain the unity of the Protestant majority and to defend it against the threat of a united Ireland. The police, civil service and judiciary were predominantly Protestant, not just because Northern Ireland Catholics were at first reluctant to have anything to do with the new state but because of the widespread unionist belief that Catholics could not be trusted. In the words of Northern Ireland's first Prime Minister, Lord Craigavon, it was to be 'a Protestant government for a Protestant people'. Until the 1960s little was done about other matters like the chronically high level of unemployment, the worst in the United Kingdom, or the social deprivation such as bad housing which affected both communities. Northern Ireland did not have enough resources of its own to tackle these problems. It depended largely on economic and welfare provisions introduced in Britain being extended to Northern Ireland – at British taxpayers' expense.

Occasionally the Protestant and Catholic working classes united to protest against unemployment and bad living conditions but the Protestant working class belief that whatever jobs were available should be given to them rather than to 'disloyal' Catholics reduced the effectiveness of such protests.

The fall of Stormont

Unionist rule in Northern Ireland was severely challenged in 1968 when the newly formed Northern Ireland Civil Rights Association (NICRA) took to the streets to highlight what it saw as unionist abuses of power. Its protest was largely against discrimination in jobs, the unfair allocation of housing by local authorities, and the undemocratic way in which local authorities were elected. Its demand was

Londonderry in 1967. Deliberate manipulation of electoral boundaries ensured that most of the Catholics were in one ward so that a Catholic city ended up with a unionist-controlled council.

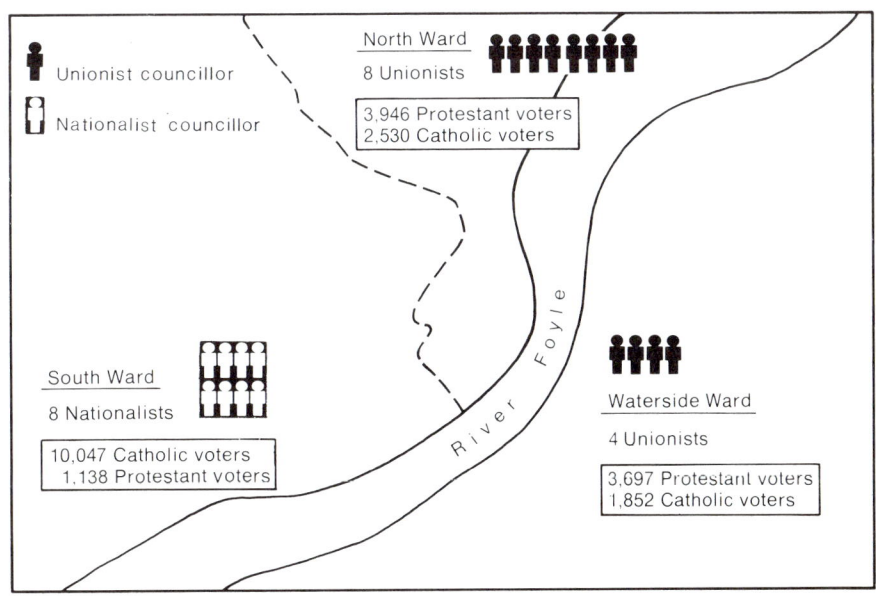

not the nationalist one of an independent united Ireland but rather that British standards of justice and democracy should operate in Northern Ireland.

LIST OF CIVIL RIGHTS DEMANDS

1 One person, one vote in local council elections
2 An end to 'gerrymandered' electoral boundaries (see page 21)
3 An end to discrimination by local government
4 A points system for housing allocation
5 Repeal of the Special Powers Act which allowed the police to detain without trial
6 The disbanding of the B-Specials, a Protestant part-time force of armed police auxiliaries

The Civil Rights movement was seen by the Unionist Government, however, as a front for nationalists and was treated as such. When NICRA tried to hold a protest march in Londonderry in October 1968 the Unionist Minister of Home Affairs refused to let it move outside the traditional Catholic areas of the city. The march nevertheless went ahead as planned and the police, armed with batons and regarding the protest as hostile, savagely dispersed the demonstrators.

Unfortunately for the unionists these violent scenes were filmed and reported by the British and international media and caused outraged concern in Britain. For the first time in almost fifty years the British Government was forced to show an active interest in the internal affairs of Northern Ireland. The demands of NICRA, which included reform of the police, received a sympathetic hearing from the Labour Government of Harold Wilson (1964–1970) and the Unionist Government of Northern Ireland, led by Terence O'Neill, found itself under pressure from London to satisfy NICRA demands. It was this pressure that ultimately led to the collapse of the Stormont system of unionist rule.

As unionist leaders were pushed reluctantly towards introducing reforms there was a growing sense among their Protestant supporters that they were being betrayed. These fears were amply expressed by the Reverend Ian Paisley who saw any reform as being the beginning of the road to a united Ireland. Tension between the Protestant and Catholic communities increased and in August 1969 it exploded as communal violence in Londonderry and Belfast. The inability of the Unionist Government to control the situation led to the British Government's decision to send in the British Army. From this point onwards the British Government was forced to accept a greater responsibility for the internal affairs of Northern Ireland.

The final collapse of the Unionist Government did not come until three years later. Increasing violence and continued Catholic lack of

Since Direct Rule in 1972 responsibility for the Northern Ireland government departments has lain with British government ministers headed by a member of the British Cabinet.

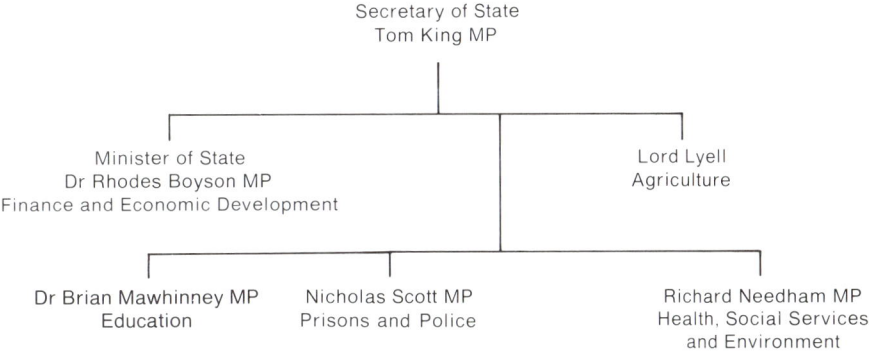

Secretary of State
Tom King MP

Minister of State
Dr Rhodes Boyson MP
Finance and Economic Development

Lord Lyell
Agriculture

Dr Brian Mawhinney MP
Education

Nicholas Scott MP
Prisons and Police

Richard Needham MP
Health, Social Services
and Environment

The Northern Ireland Office in January 1986

confidence in those security forces controlled by the Unionist Government, such as the police, led the British Conservative Government of Edward Heath (1970–1974) to take complete charge of security themselves. Rather than agree to this further reduction in their authority the Unionist Government resigned and the Stormont Parliament was suspended.

STORMONT PRIME MINISTERS 1921–72

1921–41	James Craig (Unionist)
1941–43	John Andrews (Unionist)
1943–63	Basil Brooke (Unionist)
1963–69	Terence O'Neill (Unionist)
1969–71	James Chichester-Clark (Unionist)
1971–72	Brian Faulkner (Unionist)

Direct Rule

The resignation of the Unionist Government at Stormont in March 1972 led the British Government in London to assume complete and direct responsibility for Northern Ireland. A British Cabinet minister,

BRITISH SECRETARIES OF STATE FOR NORTHERN IRELAND

1972–73	William Whitelaw (Conservative)
1973–74	Francis Pym (Conservative)
1974–76	Merlyn Rees (Labour)
1976–79	Roy Mason (Labour)
1979–81	Humphrey Atkins (Conservative)
1981–84	James Prior (Conservative)
1984–85	Douglas Hurd (Conservative)
1985–	Tom King (Conservative)

William Whitelaw, was despatched to Belfast to carry out the functions previously performed by the unionist prime minister of Northern Ireland and the various Stormont government departments were shared out among a number of British junior ministers responsible to him. This system of government was similar to that in Scotland and Wales, except that in Northern Ireland's case none of the ministers had local constituencies.

'Direct Rule', as this system is called, was intended to be temporary. It was hoped that it would establish Catholic confidence in the impartiality of government and allow time for Protestant and Catholic communities to agree on a form of locally elected government in Northern Ireland which both could support.

An attempt was made in 1973 at Sunningdale in Berkshire to reach agreement between the elected representatives of the two communities. An assembly was to be elected, similar to the old Stormont Parliament, but the government was to be made up of both Protestant and Catholic members. The *power-sharing Executive*, as it became known, survived for five months. The leader of the Executive was the previous Stormont Prime Minister and leader of the Ulster Unionist Party, Brian Faulkner, and his deputy was Gerry Fitt, then leader of the main Catholic party, the Social Democratic and Labour Party (SDLP). Other unionist politicians, however, particularly the Reverend Ian Paisley, denounced the presence of nationalists in government and saw the Executive as the first step to a united Ireland. In May 1974 unionist opposition to the Executive led to a general strike supported by key workers in power stations. Loyalist paramilitaries mounted road blocks and economic life was brought to a standstill. Unionist members of the Executive resigned. The newly elected British Labour Government abandoned power-sharing and returned to Direct Rule.

The most recent attempt to reach agreement on a locally elected government was in 1982, when James Prior, the Secretary of State for Northern Ireland, introduced his plan for 'Rolling Devolution'. An assembly was elected which was to have the power to question the British ministers responsible for Northern Ireland. Its ability gradually to take over government itself was to depend on agreement between Protestant and Catholic representatives. This has so far proved impossible to achieve since the main Catholic party (the SDLP) has refused to take its seats. In these circumstances Direct Rule has continued.

Topics for discussion

1 How did the Ulster Unionist Party manage to stay in government for over fifty years despite the high level of unemployment in Northern Ireland?
2 What were the demands of the Civil Rights movement in 1968? Why did the unionists oppose them?
3 How does Direct Rule differ from the previous Stormont system of government?
4 Explain the probable attitude in 1972 to the introduction of Direct Rule of: (a) Protestants and (b) Catholics in Northern Ireland.
5 What objections might be made in Northern Ireland against (a) Majority Rule and (b) power-sharing? Which is the more democratic system in your view?

3   Political parties

A political party has its own ideas about the policies government should adopt and its aim is to get into power in order to put its own ideas into practice. In democratic societies parties try to achieve power by standing for election.

Political parties in Britain usually differ over government policies, for example whether taxes should be increased or nuclear weapons abolished. In Northern Ireland, however, the parties differ mostly over the organisation of government itself and whether the people should be British or Irish. These issues are much more basic and the divisions between the parties, are, therefore, much more deep-rooted.

Unionism

The majority of people in Northern Ireland support parties which could be called unionist and almost all unionist voters are Protestants. Unionists believe that Northern Ireland should remain part of the United Kingdom and that its British identity should be preserved. They are opposed to any attempt to bring about unity between Northern Ireland and the Irish Republic; they believe that this would rob them of their 'Britishness' and lead them to be dominated by the Roman Catholic Church. The ban on divorce in the Irish Republic is often quoted as an example of the powerful influence of the Roman Catholic Church in that country. Only in 1985 was legislation eventually passed in the Republic permitting the sale of contraceptives to those over eighteen, and even that was almost defeated after fierce opposition from Catholic Church leaders. Such attempts by many in the Republic to have state law reflect the moral teachings of the Catholic Church has always fuelled Northern Protestant opposition to a united Ireland.

Unionists see the problem in Northern Ireland as a security one, namely how to defeat the IRA. They believe that this can be done by backing tougher measures like restoring the death penalty for murder, increasing police and military activity in nationalist areas and closing the border with the Irish Republic except at main roads.

So far the unionist parties have been opposed to *political* solutions which would force them to share power with nationalist politicians whose aim, like that of the IRA, is a united Ireland. They also oppose

Unionist election leaflets:
(a) Official Unionist Party
(b) Democratic Unionist Party

a   b

any involvement by the Irish Republic in the internal affairs of Northern Ireland.

Differences within unionism

The main unionist parties are the Official Unionist Party (OUP) and the Democratic Unionist Party (DUP). The Official Unionist Party was the party which controlled government at Stormont from 1921 to 1972 and sees itself as the respectable and law-abiding face of Ulster unionism. It has remained the chief voice of unionists in the British House of Commons where it still holds most of Northern Ireland's seventeen seats.

The principal policy of the Official Unionist Party is to maintain the union with Britain at any cost. Ideally it would like to return to the old Stormont system where government in Northern Ireland was controlled by the unionist majority. But this is less important to it than keeping Northern Ireland British. Some within the party, like the South Down MP Enoch Powell, would like to see Northern Ireland governed as if it were an English county, like Yorkshire. This is known as the *integration view*.

The Democratic Unionist Party was formed by the Reverend Ian Paisley in 1971 at a time when the Official Unionist Government was being forced to introduce reforms to meet Catholic grievances. The DUP, which is dominated by its leader, Ian Paisley, presents itself as the uncompromising face of unionism. Its distrust of the intentions of the British Government has often led it to threaten to take the law into its own hands as when Ian Paisley organised a 'Third Force' of armed volunteers in 1981 to catch terrorists. The DUP is much keener than the OUP to retore power to local politicians and his unionist critics accuse Ian Paisley of wanting an independent Ulster in which he would be prime minister.

Nationalism

Most of the Catholics in Northern Ireland support parties which could be termed nationalist. They support the idea of unity with the Irish Republic for they believe themselves to be Irish rather than British.

Nationalists see the problem in Northern Ireland as a political one. They regard the IRA as the symptom rather than the cause of the conflict. It is believed that the conflict between the Protestants and Catholics, unionists and nationalists, will always exist so long as Ireland remains divided and unionists refuse to admit their Irishness.

All nationalist parties are completely opposed to the return of unionist Majority Rule in Northern Ireland and believe that the British Government has a responsibility to persuade the unionists to accept a united Ireland.

SDLP press conference with party leader John Hume (left) and deputy leader Seamus Mallon (right). The SDLP seeks Irish unity by peaceful means.

Differences within nationalism

The two chief nationalist parties are the Social Democratic and Labour Party and Sinn Fein and between them they attract the votes of most of the Catholic minority. The SDLP was formed in 1970 to push through the demands of the civil rights movement but since then it has come to believe that peace and justice can only be achieved in a united Ireland. Unlike the IRA, it believes that this can only be obtained with the consent of the unionists, not by violence. In the SDLP view unionists must be persuaded, not bombed, into a united Ireland.

The SDLP, led by Gerry Fitt, took part in the power-sharing Executive in 1974. But the unionist rejection of power-sharing has led the SDLP, now led by John Hume, to by-pass the unionists and put its faith in closer relations between the governments in London and Dublin as a way of overcoming unionist attitudes.

Sinn Fein is the political wing of the IRA and it believes that Irish unity can only be achieved when the British Army and Government are forced by the IRA to withdraw from Northern Ireland. The only persuasion that it believes will work on unionists and the British Government is 'armed resistance', involving the killing of members of the police, army and judiciary.

In 1981 Sinn Fein decided to stand in elections to challenge the SDLP's right to speak for the nationalist community. So far it has succeeded in winning the votes of about a third of Catholics, many of them young voters living in areas where the police and army are highly unpopular. But despite its electoral successes Sinn Fein still believes that it will be military struggle not elections that will achieve Irish unity.

Sinn Fein leader Gerry Adams (right) and the party's candidate in the 1984 Euro-election, Danny Morrison (left). Sinn Fein support the IRA campaign and demand immediate British withdrawal.

Alliance Party, led by John Cushnahan (centre), appeals to both communities.

Cross-community politics

Not all political parties in Northern Ireland draw their support predominantly from one section of the community. A few put forward policies designed to attract the support of both Protestants and Catholics.

One such party is the Alliance Party which was formed in 1970. Its policy is to move Northern Ireland away from sectarian politics and to develop partnership in government between Protestants and Catholics. The party took part in the power-sharing Executive of 1974 and still believes that power-sharing is the only solution to the Northern Ireland conflict. Its support has ranged from 5 per cent to 14 per cent of the votes cast.

Another party which attempts to appeal to both communities is the Workers Party, once the political wing of the now inactive Official IRA. Unlike the Provisional IRA the more marxist Official IRA took the view that the armed struggle was only reinforcing sectarian divisions among the Northern working classes. It largely suspended its military activities in 1972 and its political wing, now known as the Workers Party, while still believing in a united Ireland, sees its immediate concern as achieving unity between Protestants and Catholics in Northern Ireland. The Workers Party is socialist, directing its message to the working classes in both communities. It usually gains about 2 per cent of the votes.

In 1985 a new Labour Party of Northern Ireland was formed with some trade union support. Its predecessor, the Northern Ireland Labour Party, had had some success in the early 1960s in winning working-class Protestant votes away from the Unionist Party but it virtually disappeared in the violence of the 1970s. The new party aims a socialist message at both communities and is independent of both the British and the Irish Labour Parties.

How the Northern Ireland parties see each other

The political parties in Northern Ireland have consistently failed to reach agreement on a system of government. Much of this difficulty is caused by the distrust and suspicion with which they regard each other.

The unionist parties suffer in the nationalist eyes from the Unionist Government's treatment of Catholics in the fifty years before Direct Rule. The refusal of unionists to admit Catholic grievances of discrimination in jobs and housing or the abuse of police powers is not likely to make nationalist parties agree to return to unionist-dominated government. Anti-Catholic remarks, such as those of the DUP's George Seawright, who publicly advocated the burning of Catholics, have simply reinforced nationalist distrust of unionists, even though he was later expelled from his party.

Similarly, the nationalist parties are distrusted by unionists. Sinn Fein is openly hated as the spokesman of the IRA and unionists would like to see Sinn Fein outlawed. The killings carried out by the IRA make unionists fear for their safety in a Sinn Fein-controlled united Ireland. Several unionist politicians, including the South Belfast MP Robert Bradford, have been assassinated by the IRA. The SDLP are also distrusted because they are seen as simply trying to achieve the IRA's goals by more devious methods. The SDLP's refusal to back the security forces fully makes them appear in unionist eyes to be encouraging the IRA.

The Alliance Party and the Workers Party suffer from being distrusted by both sides. Their acceptance that at the moment the majority of people in Northern Ireland want to remain in the United Kingdom makes them appear to nationalists as unionist parties. Yet the Alliance Party's belief in letting nationalist politicians have a share in government and the Workers Party's previous links with the Official IRA make them both highly suspect in unionist circles.

Topics for discussion

1 How are parties in Northern Ireland different from those in Britain?
2 Explain the differences between
    (a) the Official Unionist Party and the Democratic Unionist Party;
    (b) the Official Unionist Party and the SDLP;
    (c) Sinn Fein and the SDLP.
3 Unionists argue that Sinn Fein should be outlawed. Put arguments for and against this view.
4 Imagine that a new Secretary of State for Northern Ireland has just been appointed. Write a letter in turn from each of the main party leaders in Northern Ireland warning and advising the new minister on what he should do.

4   Elections

The chief means by which political parties seek power in democratic societies is by standing for election. In this way they can demonstrate how much public support their policies have and, if their candidates are successful, they can claim to represent the public in local councils or the national parliament. In Britain the party which wins the most seats in Parliament will also have the opportunity to form the government. So, government is seen to be chosen by the people and most voters will accept the result, even if they voted for one of the losing parties.

For elections to succeed in giving government a wide degree of popular acceptance several conditions are necessary. Firstly, elections must be fair and be seen as fair. In Britain most people respect the electoral process, even though the Liberals and the Social Democratic Party (SDP) are unhappy with the system used.

Secondly, the elections must lead to real power and influence for those elected. In Britain, at both national and local levels, the majority party after an election expects the power to put its policies into effect. Opposition parties and representatives also expect to be listened to seriously and carefully, and, at times, this can lead to policies being modified. Elections in Britain are therefore seen as a democratic means by which the people can shape their own government.

Finally, the successful party must be prepared to take into account the interests of the whole community and not just the one section which voted it into power. Only under these circumstances will those who voted for unsuccessful candidates gracefully accept defeat. In Britain the main parties draw their support from a wide cross-section of the community. This helps the elected government to present itself as a truly national party.

In Northern Ireland it seems to many that these conditions are absent.

Fair elections and the Northern Ireland experience

During the Civil Rights campaign in the 1960s two major complaints were about the unreformed local government franchise and unfair constituency boundaries. The restricted local government franchise meant that only local ratepayers could vote in local government elections. Since Catholics were less likely than Protestants to own property this also meant that in practice unionists were over-represented on local councils.

Unfair constituency boundaries, better known as 'gerrymandering', had much the same effect. By drawing the local ward boundaries in a particular way unionists in Londonderry were able to maintain a majority on the local council despite the fact that most of the voters were nationalists (see the map on page 9). But as a result of the Civil Rights campaign both the local government franchise and the local government boundaries were reformed in 1969.

A continuing threat to fair elections in Northern Ireland is, however, the high incidence of elector personation in certain areas. Although it is a criminal offence to do so, some people vote several times in the same election by impersonating other voters. In marginal constituencies like Fermanagh and South Tyrone it is often said that 'the dead walk' at elections, meaning that the votes of dead people are used, and in a close contest this may affect the result.

Ian Paisley, leader of the Democratic Unionist Party, during an election campaign. Election results in Northern Ireland always show a unionist majority.

A more serious threat to the value of the election is the abstentionist attitude of a significant section of the electorate and of some political parties. Until Sinn Fein seriously canvassed for votes in 1981 large sections of the nationalist community regularly boycotted elections. This was a traditional protest against the partition of Ireland. Extreme nationalist parties like Sinn Fein, even if elected, still refuse to take their seats except on local councils. This abstentionist attitude of both voters

Even if the Polling Station staff know you, you cannot vote without one of these documents.

ISSUED BY THE NORTHERN IRELAND OFFICE

In an attempt to stop personation the government introduced a law in 1985 requiring Northern Ireland voters to produce identification. Although this stopped personation in the 1985 local council elections the parties claimed that between 5 and 10 per cent of genuine voters had been turned away at the polls because they did not possess one of the limited number of approved documents: a driving licence, passport, allowance book, medical card or marriage certificate (in certain circumstances).

and parties may seem foolish but it is part of a serious political protest.

When a convicted member of the IRA, Bobby Sands, was elected as Westminster MP for Fermanagh and South Tyrone in 1981 the British Government decided that this was making a mockery of elections and passed a law to prevent prisoners and even ex-prisoners from becoming candidates in future. The danger of doing this, however, is that it may be counterproductive and only serve to undermine the appearance of a free election.

Bobby Sands was elected as Westminster MP for Fermanagh and South Tyrone in April 1981 while on hunger strike in the Maze Prison. The election of Sands, a member of the IRA, was used to embarrass the British Government and to highlight the IRA prisoners' demand for political status. The constituency had a tradition of electing abstentionist MPs.

Electoral systems

Another measure of a fair election is whether the system used produces results which roughly reflect the way people voted. Britain uses the system called 'first-past-the-post' under which the candidate with the largest number of votes becomes the sole representative for the constituency and the runners-up get nothing. In the past this system has tended to favour the larger parties in Britain like Labour and Conservative and to operate against smaller national parties like the Liberals and the SDP.

Northern Ireland uses the 'first-past-the-post' system in electing its seventeen MPs to the Westminster Parliament and its effect is generally to the advantage of the unionist parties. Under this system unionist parties have rarely lost more than two of Northern Ireland's Westminster seats at any one time despite having only about 60 per cent of the votes cast. This is partly because of the greater divisions among

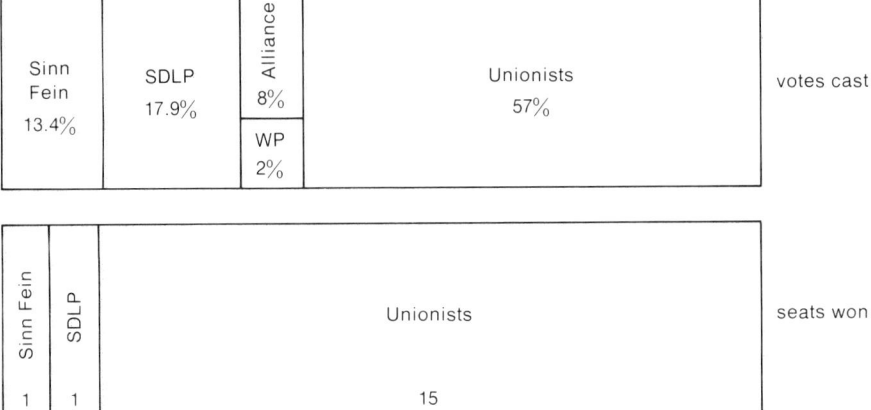

1983 General Election fought on the 'first-past-the-post' system. This system exaggerates the actual support for the largest party by making it difficult for minority parties to win seats. In Northern Ireland this means that Catholics are badly underrepresented at Westminister.

anti-unionists but it is also because it is very difficult for a permanent minority ever to win a seat under a system of 'first-past-the-post'.

To help the Catholic community secure fairer representation the British Government introduced a system of proportional representation in Northern Ireland in 1973 for use in all elections except Westminster elections. The form of proportional representation used is called the 'single transferable vote' system. This system uses multi-member constituencies and allows voters to list candidates in order of preference (1,2,3,4 . . . .). A quota of votes is fixed. This is the total a candidate must get to be elected. The surplus votes of successful candidates, and those of candidates eliminated because they were bottom of the poll, are transferred to the second preferences of voters until all the seats are filled. In this way no votes are wasted.

In the election to the European Community Parliament, for example, Northern Ireland forms a single constituency with three MPs elected under proportional representation. In practice this has ensured that at least one of the three seats will be won by someone representing the anti-unionist tradition, whereas under 'first-past-the-post' all three seats would probably go to unionists.

How much power?

One of the major differences between elections in Britain and those in Northern Ireland is that in the latter there is very little power to be

EUROPEAN PARLIAMENT ELECTION

Electorate 1,065,353; Valid vote 685,317; Spoiled votes 11,654; Percentage poll 65.42%; Quota 171,330.

FIRST COUNT

I. Paisley (DUP)	230,251
J. Hume (SDLP)	151,399
J. Taylor (Off.Un.)	147,169
D. Morrison (SF)	91,476
D. Cook (All.)	34,046
J. Kilfedder (Ass. Speaker)	20,092
S. Lynch (WP)	8,712
C. McGuigan (Ecology)	2,172

Elected: Ian Paisley

SECOND COUNT

Distribution of Paisley's surplus

Hume	(+265)	151,665
Taylor	(+38,545)	185,714
Morrison	(+49)	91,525
Cook	(+846)	34,892
Kilfedder	(+18,201)	38,293
Lynch	(+101)	8,813
McGuigan	(+64)	2,236

Elected: John Taylor
Eliminated: McGuigan and Lynch

THIRD COUNT

Distribution of Lynch's and McGuigan's votes

Hume	(+4,646)	156,310
Morrison	(+1,119)	92,644
Cook	(+2,509)	37,401
Kilfedder	(+560)	38,854

No candidate reached quota.
Eliminated: Kilfedder and Cook.

FOURTH COUNT

Distribution of Cook's and Kilfedder's votes

Hume	(+26,946)	183,256
Morrison	(+435)	93,080

Elected: John Hume

Except for Westminster elections Northern Ireland uses a form of proportional representation called the 'Single Transferable Vote'. In the 1984 Euro-election Northern Ireland, acting as a single constituency, had to elect three Euro-MPs. The successful candidates had only to win a quarter of the votes, made up of first and lower preferences transferred from successful or eliminated candidates. The surplus votes of Paisley, who was the first to be elected, were transferred to the second preferences of DUP voters, thus electing Taylor. Hume was finally elected with the help of the transferred second preferences of the Alliance voters after Cook had been eliminated.

gained by winning. Local councils in Northern Ireland have even fewer responsibilities than those in Britain – basically parks, cemeteries and refuse collection. Nor can any of Northern Ireland's seventeen MPs hope to serve in a British Government since they do not belong to the main British parties. They make little impact on a House of Commons of 650 members and only in the exceptional case of their being able to hold the balance of power between the main British parties, as in the 1976–79 period, can they hope to exert much influence.

Since the suspension of the Stormont Parliament in 1972 and the collapse of the power-sharing Executive in 1974 there has been no locally-elected Northern Ireland Government. The Northern Ireland Assembly elected in 1982 has so far been given only consultative powers and this has increased the sense among some that elections are futile.

The interpretation of election results in Northern Ireland

In practice all elections in Northern Ireland, whether for a local council or the British Parliament, are used to restate established positions on the

Party	1982 Northern Ireland Assembly Election (PR) turnout: 61.2%		1983 British General Election turnout: 76.3%		1984 European Parliament Election (PR) turnout: 65.4%		1985 Northern Ireland Local Council Elections (PR) turnout: 60.2%	
	% of votes cast (1st pref.)	number of seats	% of votes cast	number of seats	% of votes cast (1st pref.)	number of seats	% of votes cast (1st pref.)	number of seats
Official Unionist	29.7	26	34.0	11	21.5	1	29.4	190
DUP	23.0	21	20.0	3	33.6	1	24.3	142
other unionists	5.7	2	3.2	1	2.9	0	3.1	14
Alliance Party	9.3	10	8.0	0	5.0	0	7.1	34
Workers Party	2.7	0	2.0	0	1.3	0	1.6	4
SDLP	18.8	14	17.9	1	22.1	1	17.8	101
Sinn Fein	10.1	5	13.4	1	13.3	0	11.8	59
others	0.7	0	1.5	0	0.3	0	4.9	22
Total	100.0	78	100.0	17	100.0	3	100.0	566

Northern Ireland election results.

constitutional status of Northern Ireland, that is whether or not it should stay in the United Kingdom. Since the majority Protestant community will vote largely for unionists and the minority Catholic community largely for nationalists all Northern Ireland elections become a ritual which always end in a general unionist victory. Candidates who fight on class or socio-economic issues, as in Britain, rarely win seats.

This is not to say, however, that Northern Ireland elections are pointless, because many important issues are being decided. One of the most important is the battle between SDLP and Sinn Fein for the leadership of the nationalist community. Sinn Fein's open support for the IRA has meant that, rightly or wrongly, any increase in their vote is interpreted, certainly by unionists, as increased Catholic support for IRA violence. In practice it may simply reflect frustration, especially among young Catholics, at the lack of any political progress and at the depressing nature of their environment.

There is a similar battle for leadership of the unionist community. Just as a vote for Sinn Fein might indicate a hardening of nationalist attitudes, an increased vote for DUP rather than the Official Unionists would indicate a hardening of unionist attitudes. The DUP, Ian Paisley's party, is generally regarded as more militantly anti-republican.

Finally, Northern Ireland elections can be used to observe the support for non-sectarian politics. Such support is admittedly small and tends to vary according to the degree of violence in the community at the time. In periods of particular communal tension support for the Alliance Party, whose main policy is power-sharing, tends to fall but the persistence of the Alliance vote and that of the socialist Workers Party is a useful measure of the fluctuating middle ground between the two communities.

Topics for discussion

1 List the number of ways in which Northern Ireland elections differ from elections in Britain.
2 How would you deal with the problem of voter personation?
3 Should prisoners be allowed to be candidates in elections?
  Put arguments for and against.
4 Why is proportional representation used in most Northern Ireland elections? How might proportional representation affect northern Irish representation at Westminster? What might be the political effects at Westminster?
5 Write a report interpreting the results of the 1984 European Election in Northern Ireland.

5   Pressure groups

Voting for political parties at elections is one way in which the citizens of a country may make their feelings known about what the government should or should not be doing. Another method is pressure group activity where groups or organisations seek to influence the government on individual issues. Unlike political parties, pressure groups seek influence rather than power and are normally only interested in one particular aspect of government policy.

In Northern Ireland pressure groups play an important role, especially since there is little opportunity for local politicians to be elected into positions of real power.

Sectional interest groups

The most effective type of pressure group is one which can claim to represent a certain section of the community. Government often depends on such groups to provide it with information about specific needs and it is usually in the government's interests to establish a good working relationship with such bodies.

In Northern Ireland the churches, business organisations and trade unions play a regular part in keeping government informed and in helping to shape its decisions. These groups represent many of the social and economic concerns of both Protestant and Catholic communities and, as a result, have access to government ministers.

The Ulster Farmers Union is one of the most important of these and makes British ministers aware of the needs of Northern Ireland agriculture, ensuring that these are properly pressed in European Community negotiations about farm prices and subsidies.

Companies arguing for increased government investment or shopkeepers and small traders arguing for changes in security arrangements in town centres also find officials and ministers ready to discuss these matters with them. Similarly Protestant and Catholic Church leaders are able to make representations, particularly on educational matters in which the churches have a strong direct involvement, and also in areas of general social concern, such as housing.

Sectional groups which do not have a large permanent organisation or routine contact with government may find it rather harder to have their

Concerned parents hold a meeting to protest against school closures during the 'Save Our Schools' Campaign.

case listened to by those in authority. Such groups tend to emerge suddenly in response to a particular problem and then disappear again just as quickly. An example of this type of group activity was the 'Save Our Schools' Action Group, formed in 1981 by a number of Protestant parents to protest against the Belfast Education and Library Board's decision to close several state-controlled schools in its area. The closures had been made necessary by government cut-backs together with declining pupil numbers (a result of population movement and a lower birth rate). The parents felt that if the Catholic Church-controlled schools (which did not have the same problem of pupil numbers) were allowed to survive then the Protestant schools should remain also. With the help of local councillors, petitions and demonstrations the parents succeeded in saving some of the threatened schools.

Another example was the Turf Lodge Housing Action campaign in Catholic West Belfast. Here in the late 1970s local tenants organised a committee to demand that the Housing Executive, Northern Ireland's regional housing authority, should demolish the area's semi-derelict flats complex and re-house the inhabitants. The committee, led by a number of strong-minded women, produced experts to pronounce on the medical, social and environmental hazards of the flats and eventually it won its case, although not all such groups have been as successful.

Promotional group activity

Sectional pressure groups, whether of the institutional or informal type, have the advantage that they can claim to represent the interests of a well-defined section of the community. Other groups, however, may be more interested in promoting a cause than representing a sectional interest and therefore may have less immediate or direct influence.

One such group is the Northern Ireland Campaign for Nuclear Disarmament which seeks the world-wide abandonment of nuclear weapons. Although there are no known nuclear weapons based in Northern Ireland there is an important NATO (North Atlantic Treaty Organisation) early warning radar base at Bishopscourt, County Down, which CND (Campaign for Nuclear Disarmament) believes makes Northern Ireland a likely target in a nuclear war. The funds spent on nuclear weapons is also contrasted with Northern Ireland's high rate of unemployment. By focussing public attention on the cost and dangers of nuclear defence CND hopes to educate public opinion and thus put pressure on the British Government.

Another promotional group operating in Northern Ireland is the Community of the Peace People. It was founded in 1976 and is one of many groups seeking to promote peace and unity between Protestants and Catholics by the rejection of violence. In its early days it held large peace rallies but more recently it has concentrated its efforts in youth and community work and the operation of summer camps in Norway for Protestant and Catholic teenagers. But it has also campaigned against the use of plastic bullets by the security forces and for the return of jury trials.

There are numerous other promotional groups in Northern Ireland like the Anti-Blood Sports Group, which has been campaigning against hare coursing; and Life, the anti-abortion pressure group. Like all promotional groups they aim to educate the public as much as to influence government.

The Northern Ireland Assembly is one focus for pressure group activity.

Methods

There are many methods available to pressure groups. The most obvious is to make an approach directly to a government department. Northern Ireland has an advantage over most of the regions in the United Kingdom in that most government departments are centred at Stormont where they are much more accessible to local people. The chances of a local pressure group being able to discuss its complaint with a minister, therefore, is much greater than it would be if it had to compete with hundreds of pressure groups in Britain for the attention of a London-based minister.

Even so, not all pressure groups are so fortunate as to have regular access to government ministers and officials. Groups which are neither permanent nor representative institutions have to rely on other methods of influence. One such method is to 'lobby' or seek the support of elected representatives. In Northern Ireland this may be done on several different levels.

An approach may be made to a local councillor, particularly if the issue concerns local amenities like leisure centres. Although local government in Northern Ireland has very little power, councillors are represented on Government Area Boards responsible for education and health. The support of local councillors, therefore, would assist a pressure group if it sought to influence those bodies.

Northern Ireland pressure groups may also approach elected members of the Northern Ireland Assembly which, through its various committees, has the power to question Stormont ministers. The Assembly has six official committees and in carrying out their

The Assembly has six committees which hear evidence from various pressure groups. They have succeeded in influencing some of the government's policies.

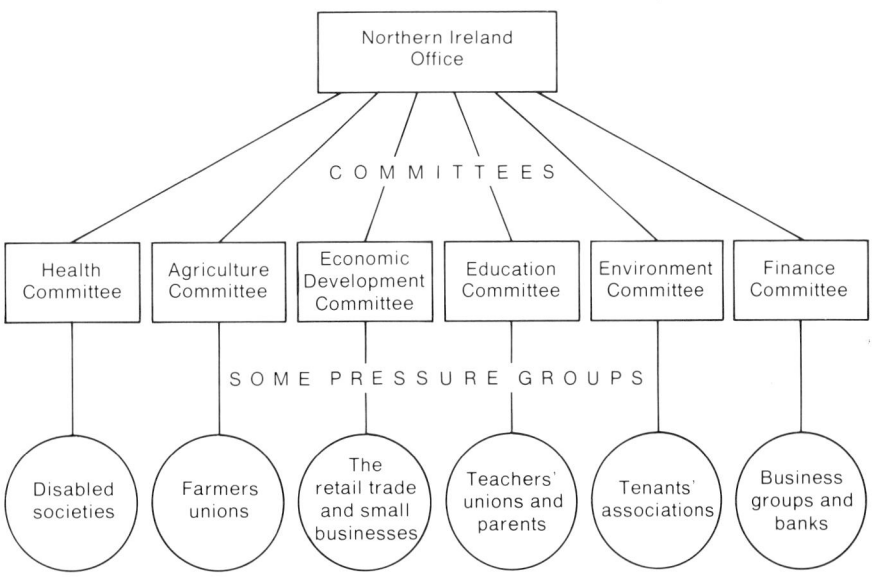

investigations into government policy and actions these encourage
pressure groups to come and give evidence.

There are also seventeen MPs representing Northern Ireland at
Westminster and these may be lobbied to raise questions in the House
of Commons or to approach a minister directly. There are also three
Northern Ireland representatives in the European Parliament and in
promoting Northern Ireland's economic interests the three MEPs rely
heavily on information supplied to them by local pressure groups.

Many pressure groups attempt to highlight a complaint by bringing a
test case to court. A favourable court decision may put pressure on the
government to review its policies. Where such a verdict cannot be
obtained in the normal courts an appeal may be made to the European
Court of Human Rights. Although this court has no jurisdiction in the
United Kingdom, by publicising a complaint it exerts considerable
moral pressure on the British Government which is a signatory of the
European Convention on Human Rights. Recognition of the legal
rights of homosexuals in Northern Ireland was won in this way.

As an alternative to court action people who feel that government

Women from the Stop the Strip Searches Committee parade with placards.
They were protesting at the practice of strip-searching women from Armagh
Prison twice daily before and after court appearances.

decisions have been unfair can go to a special Northern Ireland Ombudsman (Parliamentary Commissioner for Administration) or to the Northern Ireland Commissioner for Complaints. Both offices were set up in response to the Civil Rights campaign. The Ombudsman deals with complaints about maladministration by Northern Ireland departments while the Commissioner for Complaints hears complaints against local councils.

The most visible form of pressure is public protest, usually by demonstrations, pickets, petitions or otherwise seeking to gain the attention of the media. Although this form of activity has had some very dramatic successes, notably the campaign of the Northern Ireland Civil Rights Association in 1968, the loudest methods are not, however, always the most effective.

There is great danger in Northern Ireland in employing public demonstrations too vigorously and neglecting other methods. Street protest can quickly lead to violence, especially if confronted by hostile opposition. Unfortunately, in Northern Ireland some of the issues taken up by pressure groups divide the community along the traditional sectarian lines, and in these circumstances street protest can increase communal tension. A good example of this was the public campaign in support of the republican prisoners' hunger strike for political status in 1981. The campaign incensed the unionist community, hardening political attitudes, while the demonstrations themselves often led to violent confrontation with the police.

Despite this danger, however, pressure group activity is important in Northern Ireland if people are not to feel powerless. When unionists feel deprived of their locally elected government and nationalists feel that they are an oppressed minority, pressure group activity may be the only way of restoring faith in the democratic process. The alternative is to resort to violence.

Topics for discussion

1 What is the difference between a sectional pressure group and a promotional pressure group? Give an example of each. Which do you think would be the more effective and why?
2 What advantages do Northern Ireland pressure groups have over those in the rest of the United Kingdom in seeking to bring influence to bear on government? Are there disadvantages?
3 Outline the possible actions a pressure group in Northern Ireland could take if it was concerned about:
   (a) provision for the disabled;
   (b) strip-searching of women prisoners;
   (c) pollution of the Irish Sea.
4 Give an argument for and an argument against a pressure group engaging in a public demonstration.

6 Security

In a society where political authority and political institutions are widely respected citizens do not normally resort to violence to bring about change. If the people wish change they seek it through their democratically elected politicians. They do not take the law into their own hands.

When the laws are designed for a community as a whole by its democratically elected politicians it is reasonable to expect that most people will obey them. If some do not they will be forcibly restrained by the upholders of the law – the police. In doing this job the police can usually expect community support as in Britain. But even in Britain during the coal strike (1984–85) there were scenes of violent confrontation between the police and striking miners. Such scenes were a reminder of what can happen when people begin to lose respect for political authority. The law was defied and police use of force, far from being generally accepted, became highly controversial.

In Northern Ireland the failure of unionists and nationalists to agree on a system of government has meant that there is no universally accepted basis of authority. Paramilitary groups on both sides act outside the law and in nationalist areas the police and army are regarded as a unionist force. With confidence in political institutions so weak the resort to force occurs with alarming frequency.

The Republican paramilitaries

One group which has resorted to the use of force is the IRA. This is an armed organisation whose aim is to bring about a British withdrawal from Northern Ireland as a first step to establishing an independent united Ireland. Commercial targets have been bombed and political figures assassinated in a direct challenge to political authority. But the IRA's chief targets have been members of the Northern Ireland security forces: the Royal Ulster Constabulary (RUC), the British Army and the locally recruited military force, the Ulster Defence Regiment (UDR).

The IRA is not new to Northern Ireland for it predates the partition of 1921 and has been active on and off throughout the history of Northern Ireland. The present campaign, which is by far its longest and most violent, began in 1970. In August 1969 attacks on Catholic areas of Belfast by Protestant mobs led to Catholic self-defence units being set up. These were soon taken over by a breakaway group of the then inactive IRA and became known as the Provisional IRA. Although appearing at first as a Catholic defence force the Provisionals soon demonstrated that their aim was to engage in a military struggle to end British rule in Ireland.

Such has been the Catholic distrust of unionist politicians, the fear of Protestant mob violence, and the lack of confidence in the security forces, that the Provisional IRA has had a fertile recruiting ground. Most Catholics reject the IRA's methods but their lack of confidence in the system of government, and the security forces, has made it impossible to isolate the IRA completely from the Catholic community.

The funeral of an RUC sergeant killed by the IRA. Over 700 members of the security forces have died at the hands of the republican paramilitaries since 1970.

The IRA, and the smaller Irish National Liberation Army (INLA), regard themselves as 'freedom fighters' rather than terrorists. Indeed many people in nationalist areas are more conscious of the terrorism of loyalist violence and the sometimes undisciplined behaviour of the security forces to which these areas are subjected.

The presence of British troops and English politicians in Northern Ireland makes it easier for the IRA to present itself as fighting against a foreign power. It is the people of Northern Ireland, however, who bear the main brunt of the IRA campaign which is designed to deprive unionists, by force, of their right to remain British citizens. Civilians, both Catholic and Protestant, have suffered directly from the IRA bombing campaigns and from the trauma of the general level of violence. Moreover, every murder of a member of the RUC, police

Members of an INLA firing party at an anti-internment rally in West Belfast.

reserve or UDR is regarded by Protestants, and many Catholics, as an attack on their community, and, if anything, the IRA campaign has strengthened the unionist resolve to resist a united Ireland.

Loyalist paramilitaries

IRA violence has received much publicity. Much less is heard about the loyalist paramilitaries. Yet assassinations of Catholics carried out by the banned Protestant Ulster Volunteer Force and other loyalist terrorist groups helped to create the fear and insecurity in the Catholic community on which the IRA has been built. Over 400 Catholics have died at the hands of loyalist murder gangs since 1969.

The loyalist paramilitaries see themselves as Protestant defence units reacting to the violence on the nationalist side. They distrust British and

The Catholic victim of a sectarian assassination. Loyalist murder gangs have been responsible for the deaths of over 400 innocent Catholics since 1969.

unionist politicians and believe that only a show of Protestant force can safeguard their desire not to be part of an Irish Republic.

The largest loyalist paramilitary force is the Ulster Defence Association (UDA) which openly parades in working-class loyalist areas and makes little attempt to conceal its threat of force. The UDA remains a legal organisation, a fact which leads many Catholics to believe that the security forces are more concerned with IRA violence than loyalist violence. In 1974 the UDA helped organise a general strike in Northern Ireland which brought about the collapse of the power-sharing Executive. More alarming is the fact that the UDA has been a training group for sectarian murder squads like the illegal Ulster Freedom Fighters (UFF) which has been responsible for the assassination of alleged members of the IRA, though usually these victims have turned out to be innocent Catholics.

Army and police

In dealing with those who defy the law or take the law into their own hands the police in Northern Ireland encounter a number of problems. One is the personal danger they face in the conduct of their duty. For this reason the RUC is always armed and is supported by the British Army and the locally recruited Ulster Defence Regiment. Yet the casualty rate is high – over 700 members of the security forces have been killed since 1969.

One consequence of being subjected to the continual risk of being

The behaviour of the security forces is a cause for great concern in the nationalist community.

murdered is that the police have to be careful about presenting themselves in public as possible targets. Detective work, therefore, tends to
be conducted by detaining people for questioning and interrogation
rather than by asking questions on the streets. Also, when
apprehending suspects or investigating an incident the security forces
are always conscious of the danger of being fired upon and have orders
to shoot first, either with real or plastic bullets, if they feel that their
own or someone else's life is in danger.

A second problem facing the security forces is the lack of confidence
which they command in the Catholic community. This often results in
Catholic unwillingness to cooperate with the police, for example by
volunteering information, and, in the staunchly nationalist areas, there
is open hostility to all branches of the security forces. Very few
Catholics join the police and the UDR has become a virtually Protestant
force.

Catholic attitudes to the security forces are influenced by the lack of
Catholic involvement in the system of government and also by the belief
that the security forces are abusing their power. Despite police and
government denials it is widely accepted among Northern Ireland's
Catholics that the RUC, the UDR and the Army have operated a 'shoot
to kill' policy against suspected republican terrorists. Often the victims
have been unarmed or even completely innocent. The use of plastic
bullets, as riot control weapons against unarmed civilians at close range,
is also considered to be excessive and unjustified. In addition extensive

use by the police of detention and interrogation powers for intelligence-gathering purposes in nationalist areas has increased the sense of harassment, particularly among young Catholic men.

No policing system can work effectively if the police cannot count on the broad support of the community. The police in Northern Ireland operate under a double handicap. Firstly, they are defending a system of political authority with which only one section of the community identifies. Secondly, their controversial use of weapons which can be lethal, such as plastic bullets, makes them appear to many in the Catholic community to be acting outside the law rather than upholding it.

Twelve people have died after being hit by plastic bullets. Six have been children. In most of these cases the involvement of the victims in riot situations has been denied by relatives.

DEATHS FROM PLASTIC BULLETS FIRED BY THE SECURITY FORCES

28 August 1975	Stephen Geddis (10) killed by Army during riot in Belfast
4 October 1976	Brian Stewart (13) killed by Army during alleged riot in Belfast
10 August 1980	Michael Donnelly (21) killed by Army during riot in Belfast
15 April 1981	Paul Whitters (15) killed in interval during riot in Derry
12 May 1981	Julie Livingstone (14) killed by Army during alleged riot in Belfast
19 May 1981	Carol-Anne Kelly (11) killed by Army during alleged riot in Belfast
22 May 1981	Henry Duffy (45) killed during riot in Londonderry
8 July 1981	Nora McCabe (31) killed by RUC during alleged riot in Belfast
24 July 1981	Peter Doherty (36) killed while allegedly throwing missiles
9 August 1981	Peter McGuinness (41) killed during riot in Belfast
16 April 1982	Stephen McConomy (11) killed by Army during stone-throwing incident
12 August 1984	Sean Downes (22) killed by RUC in its attempts to disperse a crowd

The plastic bullet, officially known as the PVC Baton Round, was introduced as a riot control weapon in 1973 to replace the inaccurate rubber bullet which had already killed three people. The plastic bullet is a canister 4 inches long, $1\frac{1}{2}$ inches in diameter and weighing 5 oz. It has a muzzle velocity of 160 mph and police and Army rules state that it must be fired at a range of twenty metres and aimed at the legs. All the victims listed were struck on the head or chest mostly from close range.

The RUC came under attack, this time from loyalists, in July 1985 when an Orange parade was banned from marching through a predominantly Catholic area of Portadown.

The plastic bullet has been considered too dangerous for use in riot control in Britain and its use in Northern Ireland has been condemned by the European Parliament and by the British Labour and Liberal Party Conferences.

Topics for discussion

1 What are the arguments for and against considering the IRA as terrorists rather than freedom fighters?
2 What difficulties do the security forces face in Northern Ireland in trying to establish order?
3 What objections are made to the use of plastic bullets as riot control weapons by the security forces in Northern Ireland?
  How might the security forces justify their use of these weapons?
4 In what circumstances do you consider it desirable that troops and armed police should be used to maintain order? What are the dangers in such a policy?

7 Justice

In order that all citizens can live in security it is essential that the rule of law should prevail. But this requires not only that all offenders against the law be brought to justice but that the system of justice itself should be seen to be fair. If it is not, then people will lose respect for law and authority.

The jury system

In Britain it is normal for those charged with serious criminal offences for which the penalty is at least three months imprisonment to be given the choice of a trial by jury. A jury trial puts extra pressure on the prosecution to prove the accused person's guilt beyond any reasonable doubt and thus it acts as a safeguard against an innocent person being convicted.

In Northern Ireland jury trials were abolished for terrorist offences in 1973 as a result of a commission of inquiry headed by Lord Diplock. According to Lord Diplock juries in Northern Ireland were failing to come to an honest verdict because of fear that the defendants' paramilitary colleagues would seek revenge. He also argued that Catholic jurors were being asked to stand down by the prosecution on account of their political sympathies, thus leaving juries with a Protestant bias.

There was a certain amount of truth in both complaints. But there has been a growing demand in Northern Ireland for the return of jury trials. The removal of the jury leaves a single judge with the sole responsibility for deciding on the credibility of witnesses and the weight to be attached to police evidence. It is argued by opponents of the 'Diplock system' that the judge is too case-hardened and less inclined than a jury to challenge the police version of events. In the Irish Republic the Offences against the State Act also allows a special criminal court to try terrorist cases without a jury. But at least in the Republic such courts are presided over by a bench of at least three judges, some of whom may even be retired.

The statue of justice on top of a Belfast courthouse looks over the barbed-wire fence which surrounds it. A number of judges have been killed by the IRA.

Rules of evidence

When Lord Diplock recommended non-jury trials he also suggested that new rules of evidence should be used in terrorist cases. Normally the prosecution must produce evidence other than simply statements made by the defendant while in police custody, especially if it is claimed that these were not made voluntarily. But because of the difficulty in persuading witnesses to appear in court in Northern Ireland, Lord Diplock recommended that statements made by the defendant while in police custody should be sufficient to convict.

Christopher Black (above with his wife) was arrested in November 1981 for membership of the IRA. During police interrogation he agreed to tell the police everything he knew and to testify in court in return for immunity from prosecution. On the basis of his evidence thirty-eight people were charged with terrorist offences and tried between December 1982 and August 1983. Thirty-five were convicted of whom twenty-two were imprisoned, mostly on Black's allegations alone.

It has been widely alleged by defendants that such statements, often amounting to confessions, are false and made under duress. But attempts to retract statements have generally been rejected by the judges. A jury might be less willing than a judge to convict on the basis of a retracted confession alone. In these circumstances the fairness of the Diplock court's decisions is not always apparent.

Supergrasses

The criticism of non-jury trials has increased further since the introduction of the 'supergrass' system. In their efforts to obtain witnesses against terrorist suspects the police have, since 1981, used the 'converted terrorist' as their chief witness. Normally the evidence of such a person, already implicated in, or even convicted of, terrorist offences would be rejected by a court as unreliable unless supported by other corroborative evidence. Yet judges in Northern Ireland have accepted such evidence. They have even done so in cases where the 'supergrass' has been offered inducements such as immunity from prosecution and even resettlement abroad. The effect has been to undermine popular confidence in the judicial system in both nationalist and loyalist communities.

Defendant	Black's allegation	Further corroboration	Charge	Sentence
Kevin Donnelly	IRA membership; illegal roadblock	None	IRA membership; participation in illegal roadblock	8 years
Samuel Graham	IRA Quartermaster	None	IRA membership; hijacking;* kneecapping	7 years
Gerald Loughlin	Officer Commanding IRA 3rd Battalion	None	IRA membership; participation in murder; conspiracy to kneecap	Life + 18 years concurrent
Charles McKiernan	Member of IRA active service unit; various operations	confession (retraction in court overruled by judge)	IRA membership; murder (2); conspiracy to murder (7); attempted murder; shooting at polling station	Life (2) + 18 years
Tobias McMahon	IRA Brigade Explosives Officer	None	IRA membership; conspiracy to murder	15 years

* Found not guilty on this charge.
(Source: Workers' Research Unit, *Belfast Bulletin*, no. 11 (Summer 1984).)

Some of the thirty-five convicted on the evidence of Christopher Black.

Bail

Another cause for concern about the operation of the Northern Ireland courts, although this applies in Britain as well, has been the lengthy detention of prisoners on remand awaiting trial. In some cases defendants have been in custody for several years and still have not been brought to trial. In other cases defendants have been found not guilty having spent over a year in police custody. The reason for the delay is often the inability of the police to persuade witnesses to come forward or of a supergrass to proceed with his evidence.

Bail, the system of leaving money with the court so that a defendant can be released pending trial, is understandably denied where the judge suspects that the defendant will not return or where the offence is likely to be repeated or witnesses tampered with. The denial of bail is normally conditional on the defendant's being brought to a speedy trial. When this does not happen the defendant is being detained, in effect, without trial in direct defiance of natural justice and the rule of law.

DO YOU THINK IT RIGHT THAT SUSPECTS CAN BE CONVICTED ON THE EVIDENCE OF A SUPERGRASS ALONE?

	Protestant	*Catholic*	*Undisclosed*	*Total*
Not right	66 (50%)	63 (90%)	23 (72%)	152 (65%)
Right	63 (47%)	6 (9%)	9 (28%)	78 (33%)
No answer	2 (2%)	1 (1%)	–	3 (1%)
	131 (100%)	70 (100%)	32 (100%)	233 (100%)

(Published in *Fortnight*, Nov. 84.)

Opinion poll carried out in Belfast in July 1984 by the Committee on the Administration of Justice.

The prison system

Those accused and convicted of terrorist-type offences in Northern Ireland are usually sent to prison. This has not meant, however, that they then cease to make any impact on the politics of Northern Ireland. Indeed, in recent years, the penal policy of the government towards such prisoners has been a source of much controversy and unrest.

One such controversy was over whether those imprisoned for paramilitary activities should be given political or special category status. The problem began in March 1976, three months after the British Government had ended the policy of internment (imprisonment

Not all uncorroborated supergrass evidence has been accepted by the courts. In December 1984 the Northern Ireland Lord Chief Justice dismissed all terrorist charges against thirty-five defendants being tried on the evidence of Raymond Gilmour, a paid police informer, whom the Lord Chief Justice described as 'entirely unworthy of belief'. Many of those released (above) had already spent over two years remanded in custody.

The Maze prison at Long Kesh, Northern Ireland's main prison, with its distinctive H-Block buildings, houses part of Northern Ireland's growing prison population.

without trial). Prisoners who were interned or convicted in court for terrorist offences before March 1976 were treated differently from ordinary prisoners by being granted 'special category' status. They were allowed to wear their own clothes and were free to organise their own activities in separate compounds, rather like a prisoner-of-war camp. However, all those imprisoned for terrorist offences after March 1976 were treated like ordinary criminals and denied special category status.

The removal of special category status created enormous resentment among those who believed themselves to be political prisoners. They could also point to the fact that they had been tried without juries and under special rules of evidence. A protest by republican prisoners began which included refusal to wear prison clothes or to do prison work. In 1981 the protest reached a climax with a hunger strike which led to the death of ten prisoners before it was called off.

The government argued that special category status had developed in a very haphazard fashion. It had been tolerated when people were interned without trial; this had now ended. The main objection, however, was that it treated those who had been found guilty of crimes such as murder, attempted murder and bomb planting, in too privileged a fashion by implying that they were political prisoners not criminals. But such was the sense of outrage in the Catholic community at the unwillingness of the government to introduce a more flexible prison policy that many Catholics who otherwise would have opposed hunger strikes and the views of Sinn Fein were driven to show sympathy with the prison protest. The result was even less respect for political authority in nationalist areas.

The issue of segregation of republican and loyalist prisoners, for their own saftey if not for political reasons, is also related to the question of political status. This has been strongly supported by some loyalist politicians, as well as Sinn Fein. But so far the government has refused to declare any formal policy of segregation, despite the threat of a loyalist hunger strike.

Another issue has involved those not serving fixed sentences. Those convicted of serious terrorist offences committed while under seventeen years of age are imprisoned 'at the Secretary of State's pleasure'; this means indefinitely. Virtually all the political parties in Northern Ireland agree that the government review procedure for such prisoners is inadequate and that there is no incentive for the latter to conform to prison rules.

Finally there is the issue of Northern Ireland prisoners serving sentences in prisons in Britain. The relatives of such prisoners complain of the expense and difficulty they have in travelling such long distances to visit the prisoners and insist that it would be more humane to transfer them to Northern Ireland jails. British Army personnel convicted in Northern Ireland are transferred to prisons in Britain. The government, however, argues that the overcrowded conditions in Northern Ireland prisons do not permit movement in the other direction. Unfortunately this has done little to remove the sense of injustice felt by the families of those imprisoned.

Topics for discussion

1 Why were juries abolished in Northern Ireland for terrorist offences? Do the advantages of juries outweigh the disadvantages?
2 What aspects of the treatment of suspects in Northern Ireland undermine the belief that a person be considered innocent until proved guilty? Explain why these departures from standard practice could have come about?
3 What are the arguments for and against granting special category status to those convicted of terrorist offences in Northern Ireland?
4 Should republican and loyalist prisoners be segregated as a matter of prison policy?

8   The media

Previous chapters have been concerned with trying to explain the nature of the Northern Ireland problem. But for most people in Britain any understanding they have of that problem has been shaped by what they have learned from television, radio and the press. The extent and nature of British media coverage is therefore a major factor in the British public's attitude towards Northern Ireland.

The media can have a powerful influence. This was seen by the way in which the BBC gave prominence in its news programmes in October 1984 to the famine crisis in Ethiopia. As a result there was a massive response of private donations and public pressure on the government to organise relief aid. Similarly, it was television and press reporting of the clash between Civil Rights marchers and the RUC in Londonderry in October 1968 which first brought Northern Ireland to national prominence in Britain. As a result the British Government began to put

Martin McGuinness of Sinn Fein was the subject of a BBC television programme, At the Edge of the Union, *which was initially banned at the government's suggestion. The ban caused a television journalists' strike but the film was finally shown in October 1985.*

pressure on the Unionist Government at Stormont to introduce reforms.

The media can help to form public and government attitudes on an issue, but they can be criticised both for unbalanced reporting and even for being too balanced. Striking miners, for example, accused much of the media of bias during the 1984 coal dispute. Yet in 1982 Mrs Thatcher, the British Prime Minister, criticised television for trying to give *neutral* coverage of the Falklands Crisis. These problems of media bias and balance are amply demonstrated in British media coverage of Northern Ireland.

Should the media be objective?

Just as Mrs Thatcher claimed during the Falklands Crisis that the British media should 'back Britain', so too most British politicians believe that the media should back the authorities and the security forces in their war against the IRA terrorists. But many of these politicians would go further and insist that nothing should be broadcast or reported which might give comfort to the IRA. This would mean refusing interviews to spokesmen of the IRA cause. Indeed, in the Irish Republic it is already illegal to broadcast the views of such people.

Unionist politicians also take the view that the media should offer no criticism of the activities of the security forces. Accusations of police and army brutality, criticisms of the use of plastic bullets and allegations of a police 'shoot-to-kill' policy should, in their view, be disregarded and media attention concentrated on the funerals of those murdered by the IRA. To allow criticism of the security forces, it is claimed, is to make the difficult job of the security forces even more difficult and give encouragement to those engaged in terrorism.

In addition, the government's security advisers argue that regular and sensationalist media coverage should not be given to acts of violence in Northern Ireland because of the disturbing effect it could have on public order there. Just as media concentration on the Brixton riots in London in 1981 led to an outbreak of 'copy-cat' riots in other English cities, so also media portrayal of a violent Northern Ireland might lead to increased sectarian tension. Many sectarian attacks, for example, are not widely reported on television for fear of encouraging retaliations.

Against these arguments for selective reporting on Northern Ireland may be found the objection that it would turn the media into arms of the state. Not only would this be a serious blow to democracy and freedom of opinion but media which are known to be government-controlled are likely to be less convincing than those which are independent and able to express different shades of opinion.

It might also be pointed out that the media have a responsibility to help explain why the present violence exists. This is not the same as justifying or supporting the IRA. On the contrary, it might be in the public interest to understand what factors have given rise to the IRA's campaign and have sustained it since 1970. Only by reporting the feelings of both communities in Northern Ireland and the attitudes of all those involved in the situation, it is argued, can the nature of the political problem which has produced the present violence be properly understood.

Have the British media been fair?

Unionist views

Unionist politicians refuse to appear in the same television studios as members of Sinn Fein, whom they regard as supporters of murder. Government ministers and most politicians of the main British political parties have also objected to appearing in the same television studios with Sinn Fein spokesmen. It is rare, therefore, for the BBC or ITV to stage discussion programmes with Sinn Fein taking part. Television has, however, made attempts to put the Sinn Fein view despite considerable political criticism for having done so.

Unionists also criticised television for its extensive and regular coverage of the republican hunger stikes in 1981 and the funerals which followed. This, in their view, was allowing television to be used to further the political propaganda of the IRA. Had the hunger strikes been deprived of publicity, they argued, they would have quickly ended.

A similar criticism was made of the media coverage of the visit to Northern Ireland in August 1984 of members of NORAID (Northern Aid), the US-based organisation which raises funds for the IRA. By following the group on its tour of Northern Ireland it was said that the media highlighted NORAID's presence and encouraged republican gunmen to stage displays of defiance for the benefit of the cameras. Indeed, the illegal appearance of Martin Galvin, the banned leader of NORAID, at a republican rally in West Belfast was deliberately staged in the knowledge that the cameras would be present.

Unionists feel that their own case is not well presented in the British media. The fears of the unionists and their determination to remain British is often portrayed as bigotry and intolerance. Even the distinctive Britishness of Northern Ireland is forgotten when the whole country is spoken of in the media as 'Britain' rather than 'the United Kingdom of Great Britain and Northern Ireland'. Maps shown on television often leave out Northern Ireland.

The scale of the murder and destruction endured by the unionist community in Northern Ireland in defence of its right to remain British is thought to be inadequately communicated by the British media. It is normally only when an IRA bomb explodes in an English city or town that the interest of the national media appears to be shown. Yet

The IRA almost succeeded in blowing up the whole British Cabinet as they slept in their hotel in Brighton before the last day of the Conservative Party Conference (October 1984). Bombings in Britain get much more publicity than bombings in Northern Ireland.

assassinations and bombings by the IRA are regular atrocities endured by the unionist community in Northern Ireland, most of which go unmentioned in the national news.

Nationalist views

Nationalists, both those who support the IRA and the majority who do not, also have criticisms of the British media's coverage of Northern Ireland. Whereas unionists object to Sinn Fein being allowed television time, militant nationalists object that, on the few occasions that Sinn Fein are interviewed, they are treated as hostile witnesses. Where the Sinn Fein spokesmen are elected representatives such treatment, it is felt, shows contempt for the thousands of people who elected them. But Radio Telefis Eireann, the Republic's broadcasting service is prevented by the Republic's law from giving *any* coverage to Sinn Fein.

Another more general nationalist criticism is that the British media, and particularly the popular press, tend to regard the IRA as an isolated group of terrorists simply needing to be crushed by tougher security measures. There seems to be little appreciation of the attitudes and conditions within the Catholic community of Northern Ireland from which the IRA springs. Northern Ireland is seen as a security problem by the media rather than a political problem.

Nationalist resentment at the activities of the security forces, for example, receives little coverage. Numerous television programmes were planned in the 1970s to examine accusations of the inhuman and degrading treatment of prisoners while in police custody. But they were either banned, delayed or censored. Yet the substance of the accusations were later borne out by an Amnesty International report (1978) and a government inquiry headed by Judge Bennet (1979).

Similarly, incidents where the Army have shot or killed innocent civilians are, in the nationalist view, either suppressed or only the Army version of the event is reported. The fatal shooting of twelve-year-old Majella O'Hare in 1976 on her way to church was briefly reported as the result of cross-fire between the Army and a sniper. There was little publicity for the fact that the Army later admitted that no sniper was involved. Such incidents, if reported, would tend to contradict the popular British media presentation of the British Army as innocent peace-keepers.

Finally nationalists feel that the media concentrates far too much on republican terrorism. The activities of loyalist murder gangs are, by contrast, rarely reported. Yet sectarian murders carried out by loyalist paramilitaries have been responsible for a sizable part of the death-toll in Northern Ireland and help explain the continued existence of the Provisional IRA. When such activities are reported by the British media they tend to be presented as a response to the IRA campaign and thus not as a cause of the problem.

Topics for discussion

1 Do you think that television ought to allow the Sinn Fein viewpoint to be presented as a balance to other views in its coverage of Northern Ireland?
2 Examine television and national newspaper reports on Northern Ireland. Do you think any of the accusations of unfair coverage outlined in the chapter are justified?
3 Find a report of an incident or political development within Northern Ireland. Re-write the report from either a nationalist or a unionist viewpoint.
4 What are the arguments for and against media coverage of criticisms of the activities of the security forces in Northern Ireland?

9   Political solutions

Direct Rule – an assessment

The arrival of the British Army on the streets of Northern Ireland in August 1969 was intended to be temporary. So too was the British Government's assumption of total responsibility for the internal affairs of Northern Ireland in 1972. Yet Direct Rule, as it is called, seems to have become permanent.

Neither British nor Irish politicians regard Direct Rule as a solution to the problems of communal violence in Northern Ireland. Yet because of the failure of the people of Northern Ireland to agree to an alternative the main response of every British Government to the problem has been to continue with Direct Rule. The danger with this approach is that British politicians, having failed to find any immediate solution, will do nothing and simply hope that the problem can be quietly forgotten.

Unfortunately the problem cannot be forgotten. Murders and bombings have continued in Northern Ireland, demonstrating that Direct Rule has failed to solve the security problem. Direct Rule has also created a political vacuum in which both Protestants and Catholics feel frustrated by their own powerlessness. Unionists distrust the intentions of the British Government and nationalists feel little attachment to the system of political authority and order. Indeed, the growth of support for Sinn Fein, particularly among young Catholics, indicates that the problem may even be getting worse.

It may be tempting for British politicians not to think too deeply about Northern Ireland but, as the bombing of Mrs Thatcher and her Cabinet at their Brighton hotel in October 1984 showed, the IRA for one is not going to let the British Government or the British public forget easily.

Alternatives to Direct Rule

Unionists are quite clear about what should replace Direct Rule. The return of an elected parliament at Stormont with the majority party forming the government would, in their view, allow local people to deal with their own problems. To meet Catholic objections they are

NEW IRELAND FORUM

REPORT

2nd May 1984

The New Ireland Forum Report *(May 1984) was drawn up by the SDLP and the main parties in the Republic, Fine Gael, the Irish Labour Party and Fianna Fail. It called upon unionists to join with nationalists in building a new Ireland in which the values and identities of both would be respected. It made three suggestions as to the new political structures by which Ireland should be governed:*

1 a unitary Irish state in which the whole of Ireland would be governed from Dublin;

2 a federal Irish state with a common government but also governments in north and south to deal with local matters;

3 joint authority over Northern Ireland by both British and Irish Governments.

prepared to have a Bill of Rights, safeguarding the interests of the minority, and equal Catholic representation on parliamentary committees.

The unwillingness of the British Government to re-establish a unionist-controlled government at Stormont, for fear of civil war, has forced some unionists to consider other alternatives to Direct Rule. One alternative is full integration of Northern Ireland with Britain, with Northern Ireland treated like an English county. This view is supported by Enoch Powell, the Official Unionist MP for South Down. From a unionist point of view it would have the advantage that Northern Ireland would be seen as a permanent part of the United Kingdom. But most unionists are not English and want some separate political expression of Ulster identity within the United Kingdom.

At the other extreme of unionism are those who advocate an independent Ulster. This has been suggested at various times by the loyalist paramilitary UDA but most unionists are opposed to breaking the link with Britain. They fear that it would be a half-way house to an eventual united Ireland. There are also fears that it would lead to a civil war without the British Army to keep the two sides apart.

The only condition on which British governments have been prepared to consider handing power back to Northern Ireland politicians has been that Protestants and Catholics should share government. The power-sharing scheme, operated briefly in 1974, is supported by the Alliance Party in Northern Ireland but is opposed by unionists on the basis that they cannot share power with those whose ultimate aim is to join Northern Ireland with the Irish Republic. Moderate nationalists have subsequently lost faith in power-sharing in the face of unionist hostility.

The nationalist alternative to Direct Rule is as clear as the preferred unionist alternative. All nationalists believe that only an independent united Ireland can produce a lasting solution to the problems of Northern Ireland. They believe that the British connection only hardens the unionists in their attitudes and that as long as the border

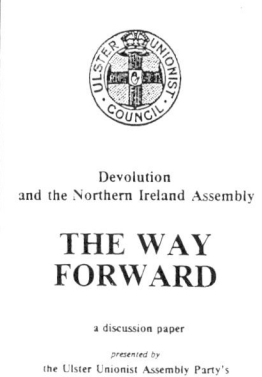

Devolution
and the Northern Ireland Assembly

**THE WAY
FORWARD**

a discussion paper

presented by
the Ulster Unionist Assembly Party's
Report Committee

Also in 1984 the Official Unionist Party issued their own document, The Way Forward. *This rejected*
1 'Rolling Devolution' as unworkable because of the condition of power-sharing;
2 the New Ireland Forum *as an attempt to take Northern Ireland out of the United Kingdom.*
But it proposed
1 'Administrative Devolution' where the Northern Ireland Assembly would be given local authority powers like education and health which are presently exercised by nominated Area Boards;
2 state recognition of Irish cultural activities in Northern Ireland to satisfy the minority's sense of Irishness.

between North and South exists a gulf will exist between the two communities in the North. The nationalist suggestion of an independent, united Ireland is fiercely opposed by unionists of all shades who fear the loss of their British identity and their domination by the Catholic Church in an Irish Republic.

Changes within Direct Rule

Recently British politicians have been trying to overcome the political deadlock in Northern Ireland by suggesting changes within Direct Rule that might eventually allow Northern Ireland politicians to work together.

In 1982 the then Secretary of State for Northern Ireland, James Prior, introduced a scheme of 'Rolling Devolution'. An Assembly of 78 local politicians was elected which was to have power to question and make recommendations to ministers in the Northern Ireland Office. Later, if there was substantial agreement between Catholic and Protestant representatives, some of the powers of the ministers could be transferred to politicians selected by the Assembly. In this way unionists would be encouraged to reach agreement with Catholic politicians.

The Northern Ireland Assembly has failed to progress beyond its initial stage, partly because most unionist politicians are unwilling to meet the Catholic demand for power-sharing. But the Assembly plan has also been obstructed by the boycott of the SDLP, the main Catholic party. The SDLP, believing that unionists cannot be trusted with power, is now looking outside Northern Ireland for a solution. It has placed its hopes for a political settlement on a closer relationship between the British and Irish Governments and the establishment of all-Ireland political institutions.

Meanwhile, faced with the unacceptable condition of power-sharing as the price of getting back into power at Stormont, the Official

In March 1984 the Irish Republic's police handed over to the RUC the suspected leader of the INLA, Dominic McGlinchey. This rare extradition was an indication of the increasing security cooperation between Dublin and London.

In March 1984 the Irish Republic's police handed over to the RUC the suspected leader of the INLA, Dominic McGlinchey. This rare extradition was an indication of the increasing security cooperation between Dublin and London.

Unionist Party has been promoting the idea of increasing the powers of local councils as a way of restoring power to the local politicians. But nationalists have fiercely opposed any attempt to re-establish unionist control by the back door. Evidence of discrimination practised by the unionist controlled council in Craigavon in 1984 in refusing to lease land to a local Gaelic Athletic Club has only reinforced that view.

Some attempt may yet be made to make Direct Rule more acceptable to nationalists. One suggestion is that the Flags and Emblems Act might be amended to allow the Irish Tricolour equality of status with the Union Jack in Northern Ireland; at the moment it can be illegal for northern nationalists to fly the flag which they consider to be their own. This small step would be no substitute for a political solution but it would be of great symbolic value and would give the nationalist minority the recognition and equality of status which they feel the unionist community denies them. Another step might be to allow Irish Gaelic to be used as well as English in street names in nationalist areas. Such gestures would cost little but would provide an important unionist recognition of the nationalists' right to be considered Irish, without necessarily threatening the union with Britain.

Anglo-Irish relations

In the nationalist view all previous attempts to solve the Northern Ireland problem have failed because most unionists and British governments have refused to consider the Irish dimension. In other words, the nationalists believe that the solution must involve the whole of Ireland and not just the North.

For Sinn Fein and the IRA only a complete British political and

Dr FitzGerald and Mrs Thatcher meet at Hillsborough in November 1985 to sign the Anglo-Irish Agreement.

military withdrawal will suffice. For the SDLP the Irish Republic's Government must be involved in the search for a solution that would allow nationalists and unionists to live together without one side surrendering to the other.

The SDLP has refused to join the Northern Ireland Assembly because it does not believe that the interests of the minority can be properly safeguarded and respected in a purely Northern Ireland context. It believes that the involvement of the Irish Republic in Northern Ireland's affairs is essential if the minority is ever to develop confidence in the political system. One of the suggestions in its *New Ireland Forum Report* (May 1984) was that Britain and the Irish Republic should share responsibility for Northern Ireland.

Unionists, however, reject any right of the Irish Republic to interfere in the internal affairs of Northern Ireland and the British Government has assured them that Northern Ireland will remain under British rule so long as that is the wish of the majority. But this has not stopped the British Government from seeking to establish a closer relationship with the Irish Republic.

In November 1985 a formal agreement was signed at Hillsborough in Northern Ireland by Margaret Thatcher, the British Prime Minister, and Garret FitzGerald, the Irish Prime Minister. The agreement established a permanent Anglo-Irish Conference based in Belfast through which ministers and officials from London and Dublin could meet on a regular basis to discuss matters of common interest, including the affairs of Northern Ireland.

The security benefits of such a relationship are recognised in London where it is believed that cooperation with the Irish Republic is essential in curbing the activities of the IRA and in gaining the confidence of the Catholic minority in Northern Ireland. It is possible that continued close cooperation between the two governments, not just on security, but on other political and economic matters, may eventually succeed in making the border between North and South seem less relevant. It is even possible that the Anglo-Irish Conference might develop a parliamentary tier that would involve British, Irish and Northern Ireland MPs.

The initial reaction of unionist politicians to the Hillsborough Agreement, however, has been hostile. To demonstrate the strength of unionist feeling against the influence of Dublin in their affairs the fifteen unionist MPs resigned their seats at Westminster and in the ensuing by-elections in January 1986 regained all but one seat in the 'Ulster Says No' campaign.

Only by assuring each of the two communities in Northern Ireland that it is not going to be dominated by the other can a solution be found. This will require patience and hard work by both the British and Irish Governments to which unionist and nationalist communities respectively look for protection of their interests. The Irish Government, in its desire for a united Ireland, must not appear to be threatening unionists; the British Government, in its support of the rights of the unionist majority, must not appear insensitive to the feelings of the nationalist minority. Only if both governments can cooperate in this task and give it their full attention can centuries of hate and distrust between the two communities in the North eventually be removed.

Topics for discussion

1 Why do few people consider Direct Rule a permanent solution to the Northern Ireland conflict?
2 Many unionists argue that there is no political solution to the conflict in Northern Ireland, only a need for increased security efforts to defeat the IRA. How would those searching for a political solution meet this argument?
3 List the main proposals for solving the Northern Ireland problem. Which do you prefer and why?
4 Why do the main unionist and nationalist parties reject power-sharing within Northern Ireland as an alternative to Direct Rule?
5 Closer cooperation between the British and Irish Governments has been regarded by many as the most hopeful prospect for a peaceful solution to the Northern Ireland conflict. What benefits does (a) the British Government and (b) the Irish Government see in a closer relationship?

Index